50 THINGS YOU DIDN'T KNOW ABOUT
The Middle Ages

**Written and Illustrated
by Sean O'Neill**

RED CHAIR ·PRESS·

Egremont, Massachusetts

50 Things You Didn't Know About is produced and published by Red Chair Press:

Red Chair Press LLC   PO Box 333   South Egremont, MA 01258

The publisher does not have any control over and does not assume
any responsibility for third-party websites or their content.

LC record available at https://lccn.loc.gov/2019931711

First softcover edition ISBN: 978-1-63440-801-1

Printed in the United States of America

0320 1P CGF20

TABLE of CONTENTS

CHAPTER 1

FEUDALISM

The Middle Ages, also called the *medieval* (mehd-evil) period, began when the Roman Empire lost power in Europe, in 476, and lasted until about 1450, a period of almost 1,000 years.

The end of the Roman power in the West led to a chaotic period in Europe, in which roaming bands of **barbarians** terrorized the countryside. To protect against this, a new system of governance called *feudalism* arose.

POTATOES AGAIN, HUH?

YEP.

1 In feudalism, powerful lords would provide land to peasants and offer protection in the event of attack. In exchange, the peasants, called *vassals*, would turn over to the lords a portion of what they grew on the land.

2 When a lord granted land to a vassal, there was a ceremony to make it official. Instead of a lease, the tenant was given a symbolic clod of dirt, called a *seisin*.

3 In some parts of Europe, individual towns that grew rich from trade built impressive buildings to showcase their wealth. An Italian town called Pisa built the famous Leaning Tower in 1173. Although it seems like, with all that money, they could have fixed the tower!

CASTLES & WARFARE

Fairy tales and fantasy stories have given us romantic notions of magical palaces with glittering towers and spires. In reality, medieval castles were military fortresses built primarily for defense against hostile invaders. Constant warfare was a reality of life in the Middle Ages, so a castle needed to be large enough to protect all of the villagers under its control, and strong enough to hold out against long, sustained attacks.

WHO GOES THERE?

4 Warfare was common in Medieval Europe, and many wars dragged on for generations. The Hundred Years War between England and France actually lasted 116 years—from 1337 to 1453!

5 Much of what we know about medieval warfare comes from works of art from the period. The Bayeux Tapestry, which is on display in Bayeux, France, tells the story of the Battle of Hastings in England in 1066.

6 Sometimes flaming arrows were shot at a castle to try to set a fire. In one such **siege**, in 1136, there was no water and the fire had to be put out with wine!

7 A common trick was to place stuffed dummies along the castle's **battlements** to make it appear to the invading army that the castle was heavily defended.

8 The most important feature of a castle was the defensive strength of its walls. In order to provide protection from attack, castle walls were made of stone and were up to 15 feet (4.5 m) thick!

9 One very effective defensive feature of castles were the meurtrière "murder holes." These small openings in the wall allowed defenders to pour boiling water and hot sand, or shoot arrows, onto the invaders below.

10 Castles had many other protective features. They were designed with narrow spiral staircases, so an invader would bang into the stone wall when he tried to swing his sword.

CLANK

CURSED SPIRAL STAIR!

CLANK

11 There were many methods to try to penetrate a castle's defenses. A mobile tower, called a belfry, was a protected stairway that allowed invaders to climb over the walls. Armored tunnels allowed miners to dig tunnels under the walls, and a type of catapult called a trebuchet could launch a 200 pound (90 kg) stone 1,000 feet (304 m).

12 Trebuchets didn't only throw stones. Sometimes the body of a dead, rotting animal was launched over the walls in the hopes of spreading disease among the castle's defenders.

PIG INCOMING!

13 Gunpowder was first invented in China, and was brought to Europe in about 1250. But for the first 200 years or so, it was unreliable for weapons. Early cannons often exploded, injuring or killing the soldiers firing them.

14 Because castles were so well defended, sometimes, instead of attacking, an invading force would lay siege to a castle, cutting off supplies of food until the defenders inside began starving and surrendered.

15 This technique didn't always work, though. Castle defenders would sometimes throw loaves of bread down at the invading soldiers. Seems like a weird choice of weapon, but it was actually a way of indicating that they had plenty of food and wouldn't be starved out.

KNIGHTS & ARMOR

There is no more familiar image from the Middle Ages than the brave knight in shining armor atop his trusty steed. Legends like King Arthur and his brave and gallant Knights of the Round Table offer a mythical view of chivalry and **heraldry**, but in reality, the life of a Medieval knight was quite different than how it's portrayed in stories and legends.

16 Most knights had at least three horses: one for traveling, one for carrying all of his equipment, and one for riding into battle.

17 A medieval warrior's most valuable possessions, other than his horses, were his armor and weapons. Soldiers and military leaders always kept them nearby, and were often buried with them after they died.

18 Knights followed a code of behavior called *chivalry*. According to the laws of chivalry, a knight must serve his king, protect women and children, never lie, and generally live by honor and for glory.

19 A knight occupied a role in European society between lords and peasants. A knight was granted land by a lord in exchange for an oath of loyalty promising to defend the lord in battle. Although when he wasn't fighting wars, most knights spent most of their time farming the land.

20 The most common type of armor worn in battle was a long, mail jacket called a hauberk. Mail, sometimes called "chain mail," was made up of hundreds of tiny metal rings linked together. Suits of plate armor weren't introduced until the 15th century, and were then mostly used in **jousting** tournaments.

21 Mail was made by hand by painstakingly weaving metal coils together. A single mail hauberk took months to make.

22 Knights in the crusades wore a white "surcoat" over their armor to reflect the sun's rays to prevent them from heating up the metal of their armor.

23 Knights didn't wear colorful coats of arms just to look cool. The system of patterns and colors followed distinct rules—called *heraldry*—and was necessary so that soldiers on the field of battle could easily identify their leader.

24 Jousting tournaments were spectacles to behold, but also a chance for a knight to get rich. A victorious knight could take the loser's armor, weapons, horse, and even hold him for ransom!

25 A knight in training was called a squire. Because a knight's armor was so heavy and cumbersome, the squire had to put it on for him, which took over an hour.

26 Not all great knights and warriors were men. In the 15th century, a peasant girl named Joan of Arc convinced the king of France to allow her to lead knights into battle against the English. Under Joan's leadership, the French soldiers **liberated** the French city of Orléans.

27 Each individual piece that made up a suit of plate armor had a specific name:

HELMET

PAULDRONS

REREBRACES

HURRY UP!

BREASTPLATE

GAUNTLETS

CUISSES

POLEYNS

GREAVES

SABATONS

DAILY LIFE

Life in the Middle Ages was no picnic. The streets were filled with waste and crawling with rats, disease and starvation was rampant, and the threat of war was never far away. If you were not a knight or a lord, daily life was fairly bleak. But, despite this, ordinary medieval citizens still managed to have pretty interesting lives.

BLECH!

28 Because most people couldn't read, shop signs in towns and villages had to be symbols of what was done in the shop. A tailor's sign might be a pair of scissors, and a bakery would be a loaf of bread.

29 In the Middle Ages most people couldn't read or write. Writing was mostly done by monks in monasteries, and was done with a quill, which was made from a goose or swan feather. They wrote on parchment, which was made from dried animal skin.

30 Many great writers of the Middle Ages didn't actually know how to write. Writing was a task performed by laborers called scribes. Teachers and priests would recite their thoughts and stories to the scribe, who would write it all down.

31 Bathing was a real chore in the Middle Ages. Water had to be fetched from a stream or well, and heated over a fire before being put in a tub. As a result, many peasants simply never bathed.

32 When they did bathe, the entire family used the same bathwater, going from oldest to youngest. By the time the younger children got a turn, the water was filthy and disgusting. This is also where we get the expression, "don't throw out the baby with the bathwater."

33 People didn't do much better taking care of their clothes. Most people wore the same clothes day after day without washing them.

34 Going to the bathroom was dangerous business. In 1325, a London resident woke in the middle of a cold night, and decided to relieve himself out his bedroom window. As he leaned over in the darkness, he fell out the window to his death!

35 A safer method was to simply use a chamber pot. These pots were emptied out the window with the warning "Gardey Loo!" (Gardez l'eau is French for "Beware the water.") "Going to the loo" is still British slang for using the bathroom.

36 Ordinary peasants were kept busy on their land, and most never traveled more than a few miles from their homes. But some medieval adventurers traveled far and wide. Italian explorer Marco Polo ventured all the way to the court of Chinese emperor Kublai Khan in the 14th century.

37 Castles and large manor houses had bathrooms called "jakes." A jake was a small room that hung out from the side of the castle wall, and the toilet was simply a bench with a hole in it. That way, waste would simply fall down the side of the castle into a moat or pit below.

38 Many medieval dishes seem outlandish to us now. An old French cookbook claimed that hedgehog meat would help people who had urination problems. Other common foods included vulture, peacock, whale, and eel.

39 Medieval diners ate some pretty disgusting food.
They also didn't have forks, typically eating with
their fingers. But they weren't complete slobs:
it was considered terrible manners to put your
elbows on the table.

40 One of the most popular medieval meals was
haggis, which is the heart, liver, and lungs of a
sheep, boiled in the sheep's stomach. Haggis is still
popular in Scotland. Yum!

41 Sometimes for a special event to surprise guests, live birds were placed in a pie crust so they would come flying out when it was cut into.

42 An Italian traveler in Russia in the 1400s found a market along the banks of a frozen river, where cows and pigs were sold frozen solid—the first frozen dinners!

43 Food was usually served on thick slices of stale bread called trenchers. After a feast, trenchers were collected in a basket and given to the poor.

44 Water in most places was unsafe to drink, so most people drank milk, wine, or beer.

45 In England a popular method for saving money was to place coins and valuables into a jar made of a type of clay called "pygg." These "pygg jars" were probably the forerunner to the piggy bank.

46 There were celebrations on some holidays. Popular forms of entertainment included dancing bears and dogs that were trained to perform acrobatics.

PLAGUE & MEDICINE

Because of general uncleanliness and lack of sanitation, sickness and disease were rampant in medieval Europe, and spread quickly. The Bubonic Plague that struck in 1347 killed one-third of all the people in Europe! It didn't help that medical technology in the Middle Ages was primitive at best. These medical facts are pretty outlandish, and, unfortunately, were largely ineffective.

AH CHOO

47 The Bubonic Plague (also called the Black Death) originated in China. It traveled to Europe in the form of rats infected with the disease that boarded ships bound for Italy. It was actually the fleas on the rats that transmitted the deadly disease to humans.

48 Brushing teeth was optional in the Middle Ages. Some folks polished their teeth with a powder made from ground up seashells, although most people just let their teeth rot, and eventually had them pulled out without the use of painkillers (which hadn't yet been invented). Ouch!

49 You probably remember the childhood rhyme "Ring Around the Rosy." It actually refers to the red rash that would appear on the skin when infected with the plague. The last line of the rhyme, "…we all fall down," is pretty self-explanatory.

50 Because of the spread of disease, there were rules about where animals could be raised and slaughtered. But it wasn't just because of disease—after a pig caused a rider to be knocked from his horse in Paris, the French king banned the raising of pigs in French towns.

WANTED
PUBLIC ENEMY #1

Glossary

barbarians: uncivilized people

battlements: a low wall with openings on top of a castle or tower

heraldry: color and design used to represent a family or group, usually seen on a shield

jousting: combat on horseback between knights, usually using long lances or spears

liberate: to set free

siege: when an army surrounds a place for a long time, to force it to surrender

Explore The Middle Ages More

Books

Boyer, Crispin. *Everything Castles.* National Geographic Kids, 2011.

Gregory, Josh. *If You Were a Kid in a Medieval Castle.* Children's Press, 2017.

Kudlinski, Kathleen. *Joan of Arc* (DK Biography). DK Children, 2008.

Pollack, Pam and Meg Belviso. *Who Was Joan of Arc?* Penguin Workshop, 2016.

On the Web

DK Find Out!
https://www.dkfindout.com/us/history/castles/

Index

About the Author/Illustrator

Sean O'Neill is an illustrator and writer living in Chicago. He is the creator of the *Rocket Robinson* series of graphic novels. Sean loves history, trivia, and drawing cartoons, so this project is pretty much a dream assignment. And it comes with castles and knights!